THIS LEFT HAND
HANDWRITING
PRACTICE BOOK
HELPS KIDS OF ALL AGES
TO START
LEARNING LETTERS
OF THE ALPHABET
AND
TO IMPROVE
THEIR HANDWRITING.

THE MAIN THING
WITH ALL WRITING PRACTICE
IS TO
HAWE FUN!

ANIMALS
& ALPHABET
HANDWRITING WORKBOOK

This workbook belongs to:

ABC

SCAN ME

TO
VISIT AMAZON'S ONE LITTLE HOUSE PRESS PAGE
AND FIND MORE INTERESTING BOOKS
FOR YOUR KIDS

RIGHT HAND   LEFT HAND

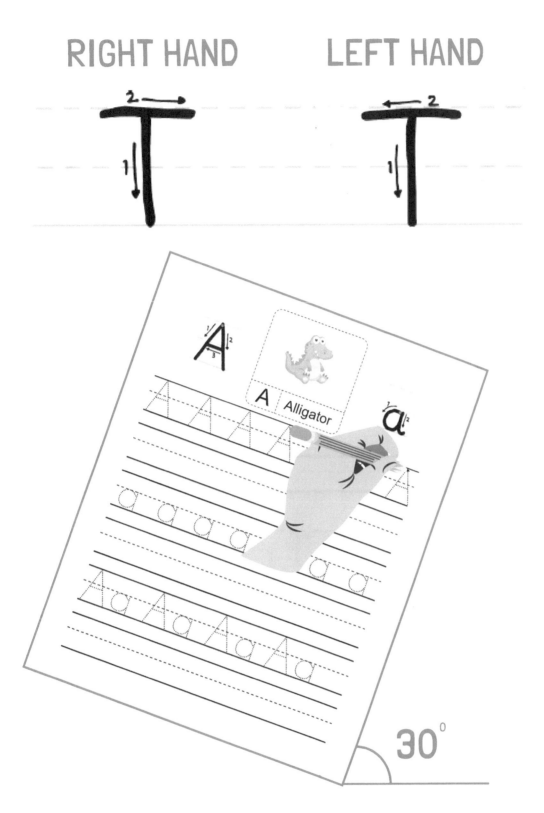

PRACTICE WITH YOUR ABCs.
WORK ON HOLDING THE PEN COMFORTABLY.
PRACTICE WRITING EVERY DAY.

A | Alligator

A A A A A A A A A

a a a a a a a a

Aa Aa Aa Aa Aa Aa Aa

FREE DRAW

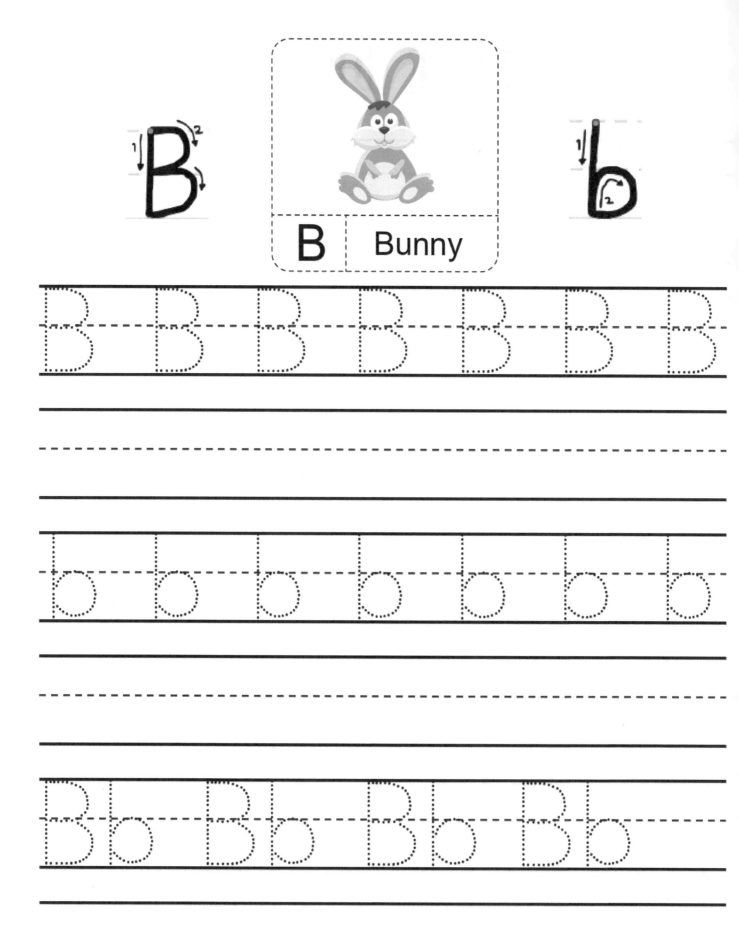

B Bunny

FREE DRAW

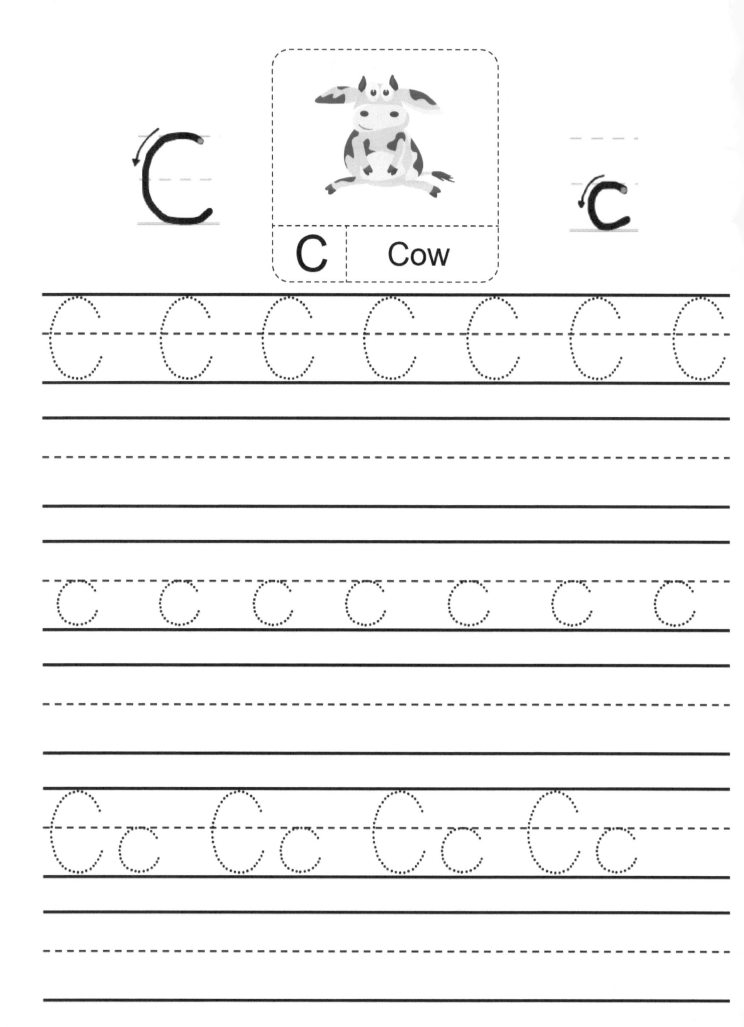

C   Cow

FREE DRAW

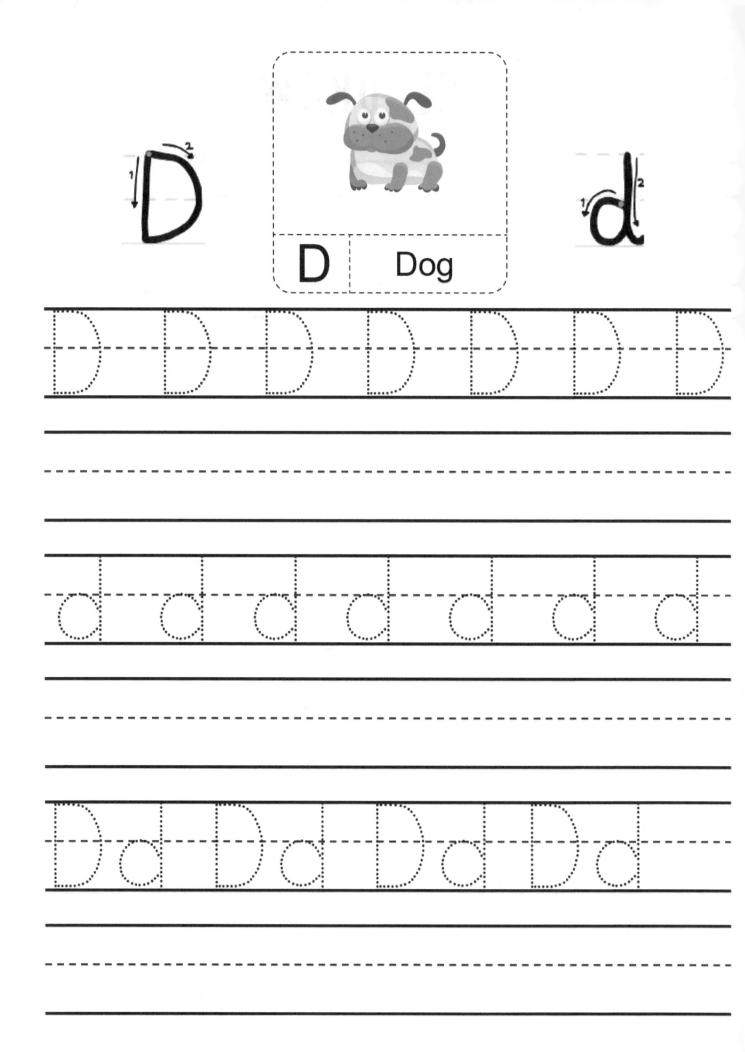

D Dog

FREE DRAW

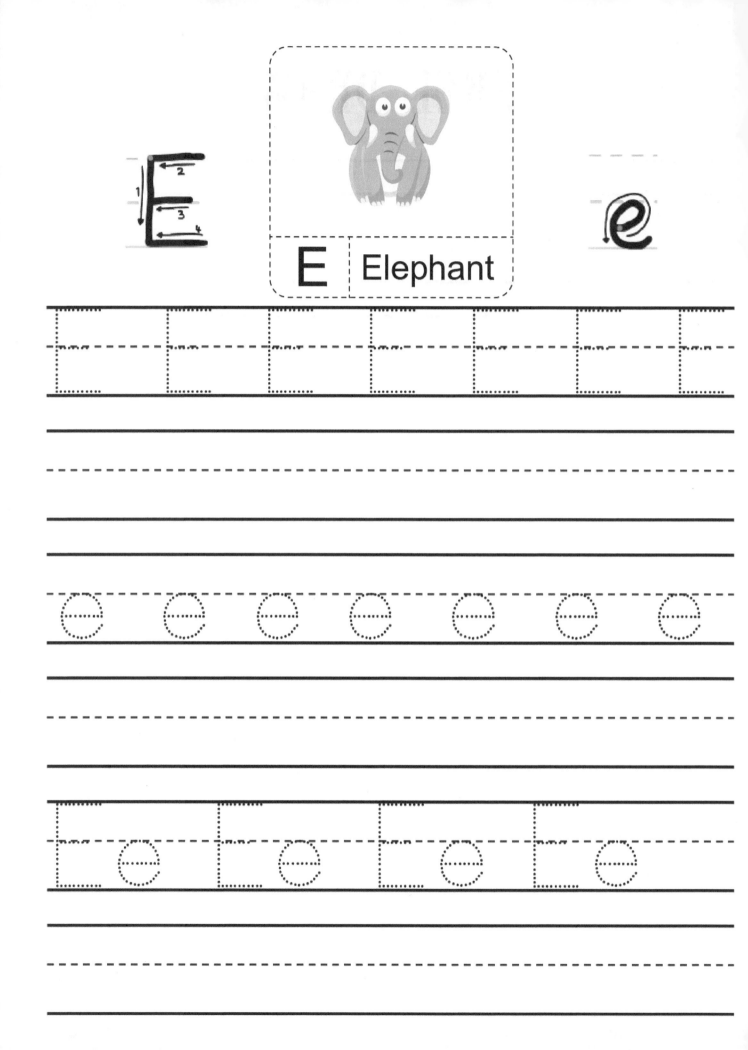

E | Elephant

FREE DRAW

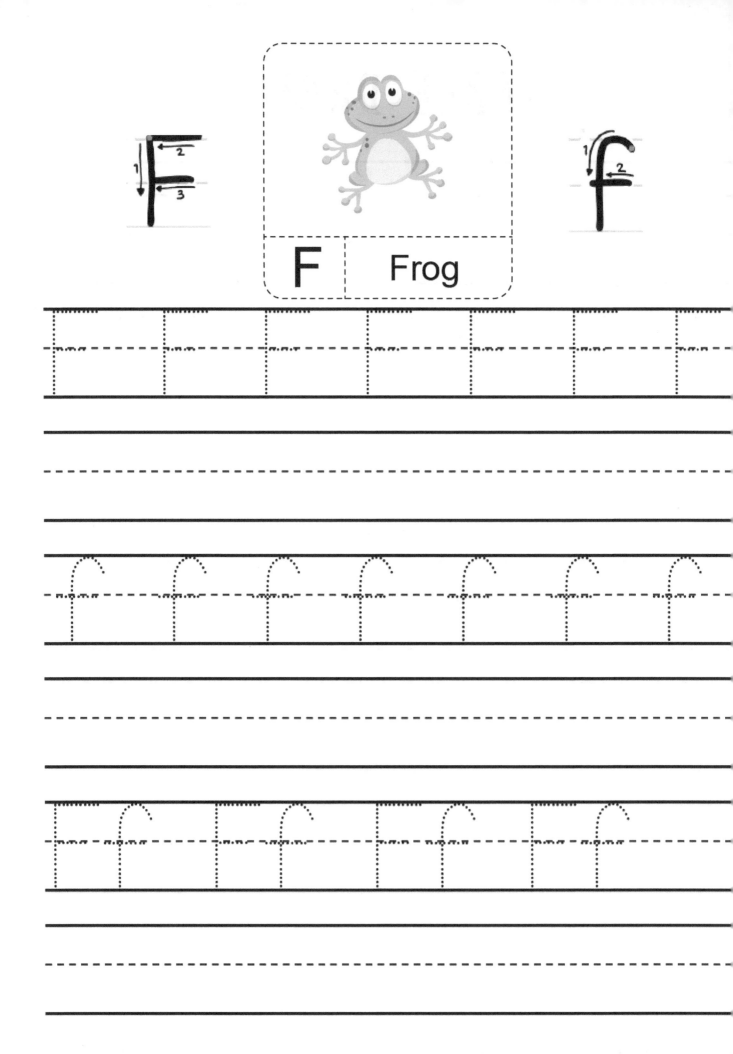

F | Frog

FREE DRAW

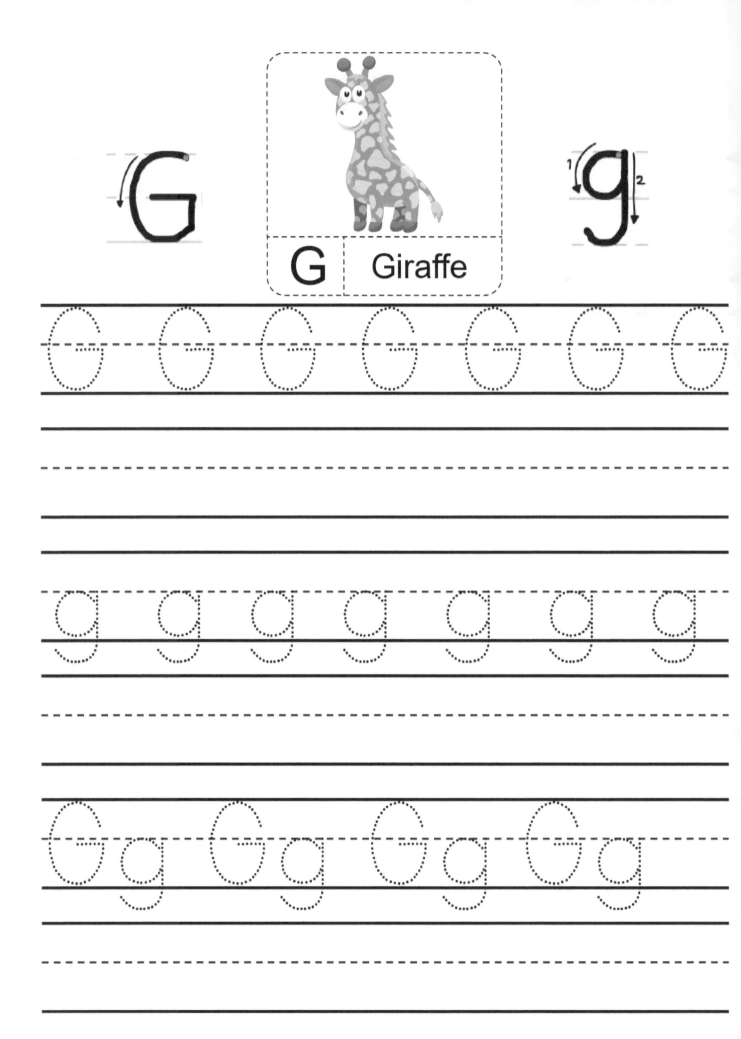

G

G Giraffe

g

FREE DRAW

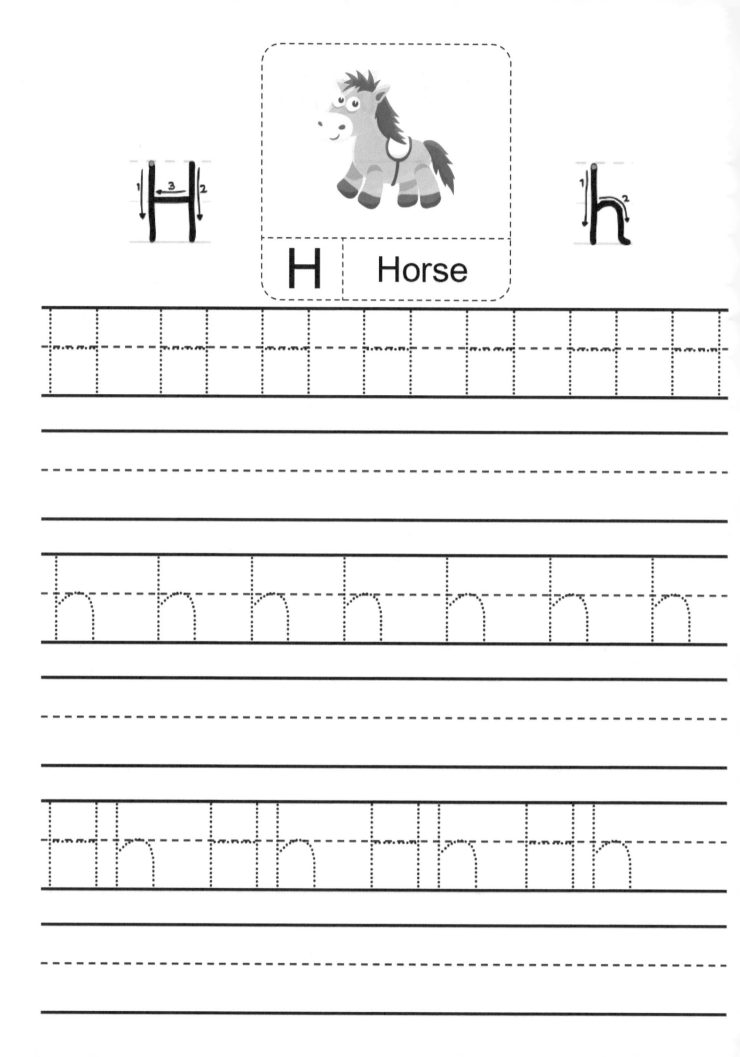

H   Horse

FREE DRAW

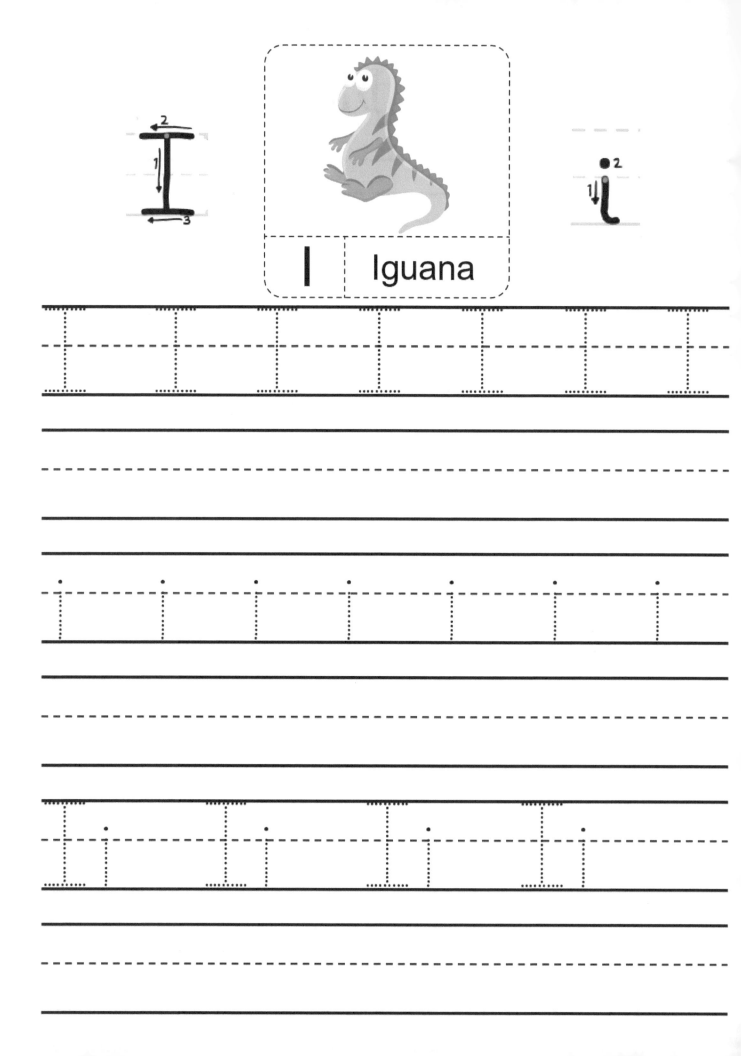

I   Iguana

FREE DRAW

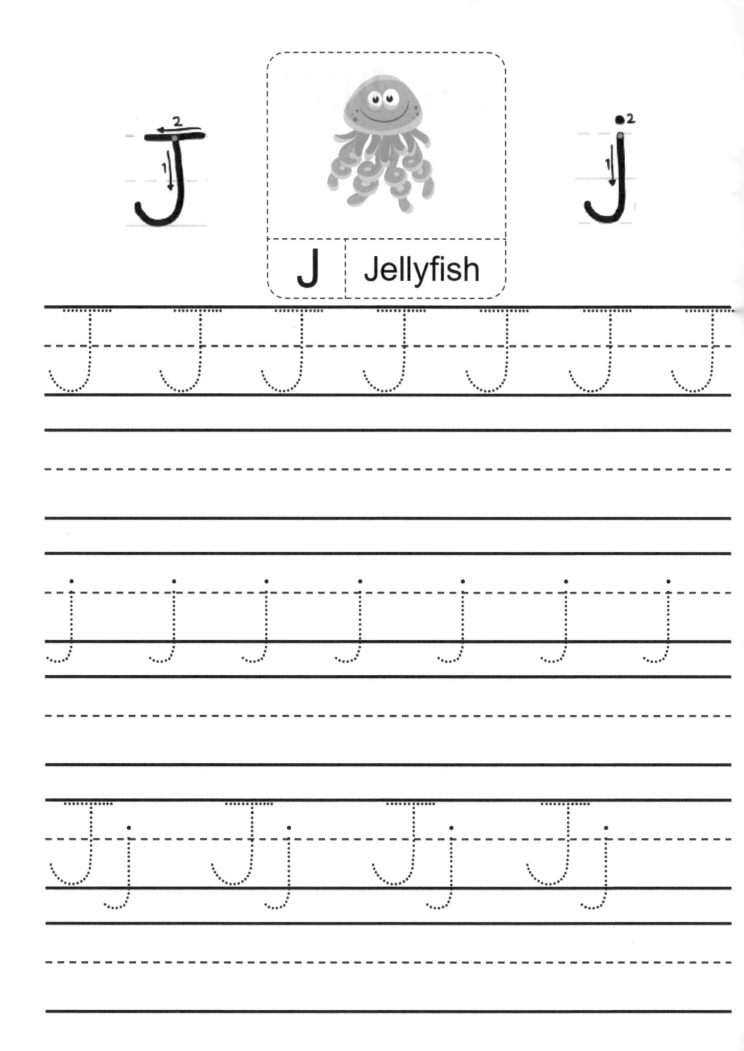

J

Jellyfish

FREE DRAW

K | Kangaroo

FREE DRAW

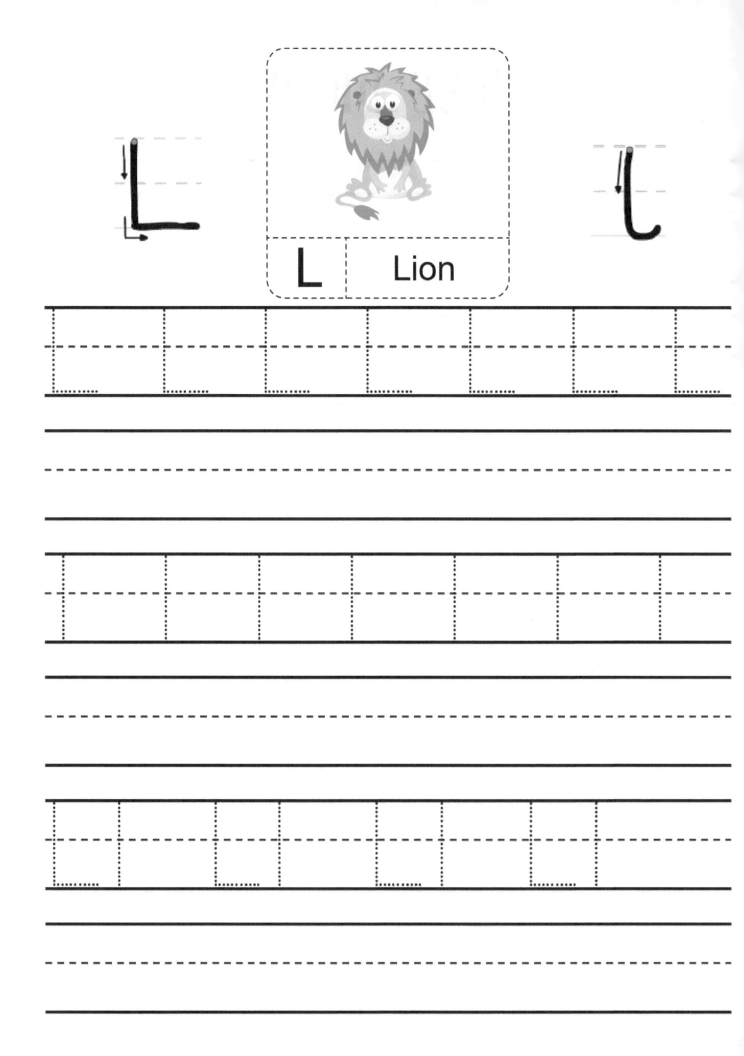

L   Lion

FREE DRAW

M | Mouse

MMMMMMMMMM

mmmmmmmm

MmMmMmMmMm

FREE DRAW

N Numbut

N N N N N N N N N N N N

n n n n n n n n

Nn Nn Nn Nn

FREE DRAW

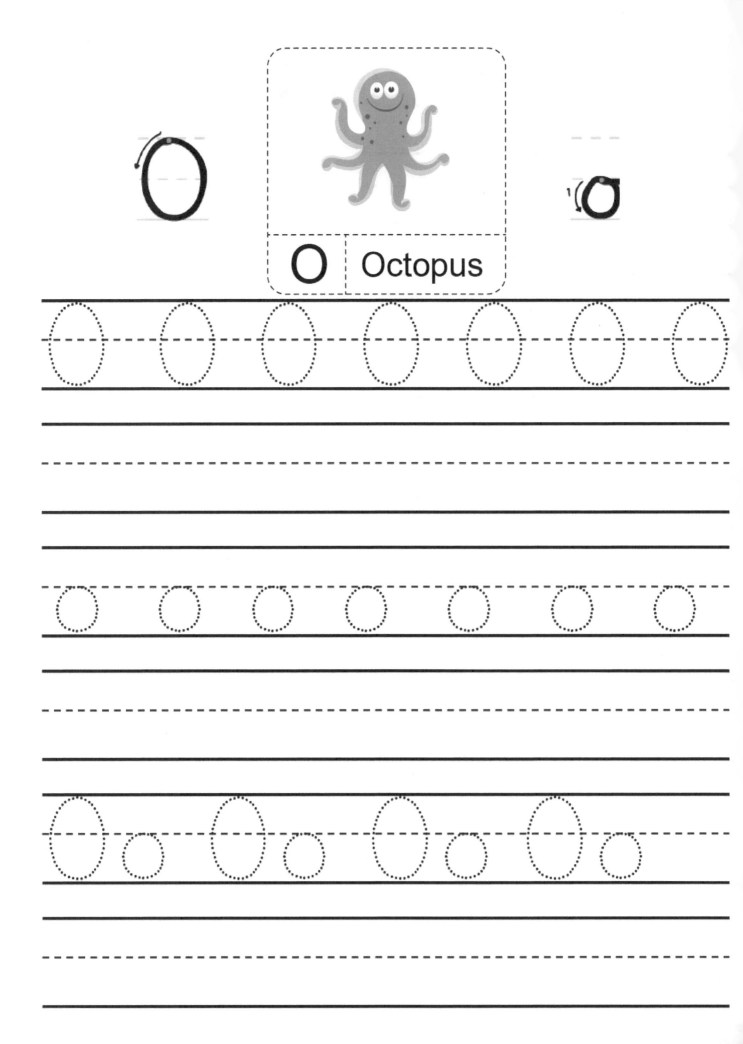

O   Octopus

FREE DRAW

P

Panda

FREE DRAW

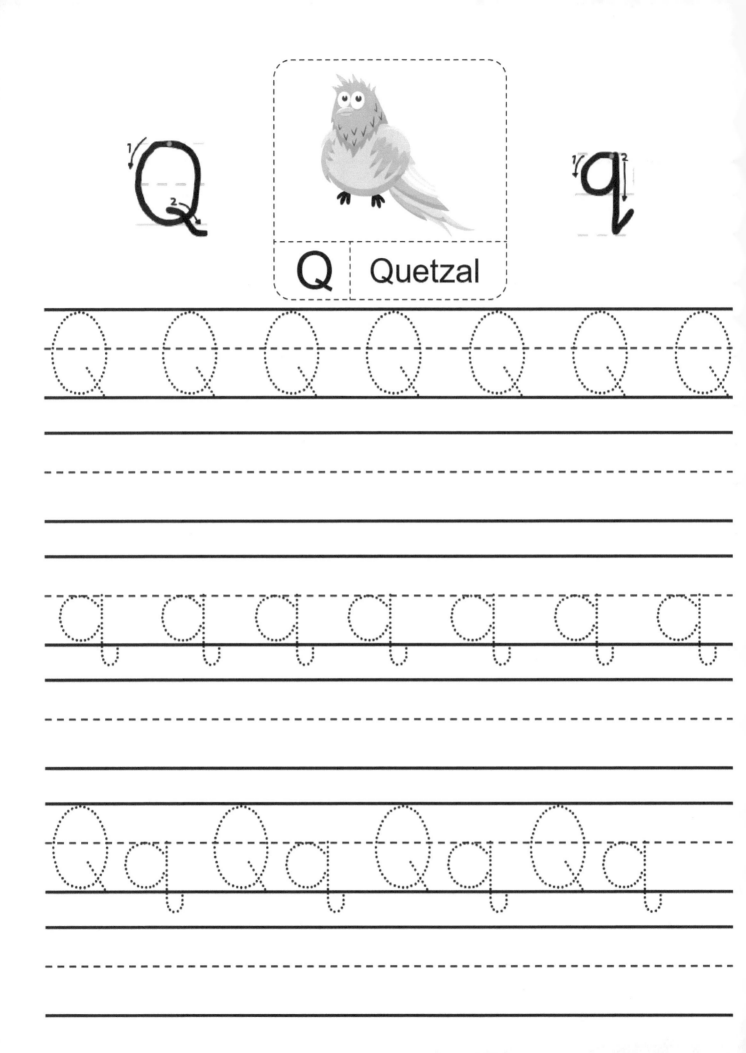

Q   Quetzal

FREE DRAW

R Raccoon

FREE DRAW

S S

Sheep

S S S S S S S

FREE DRAW

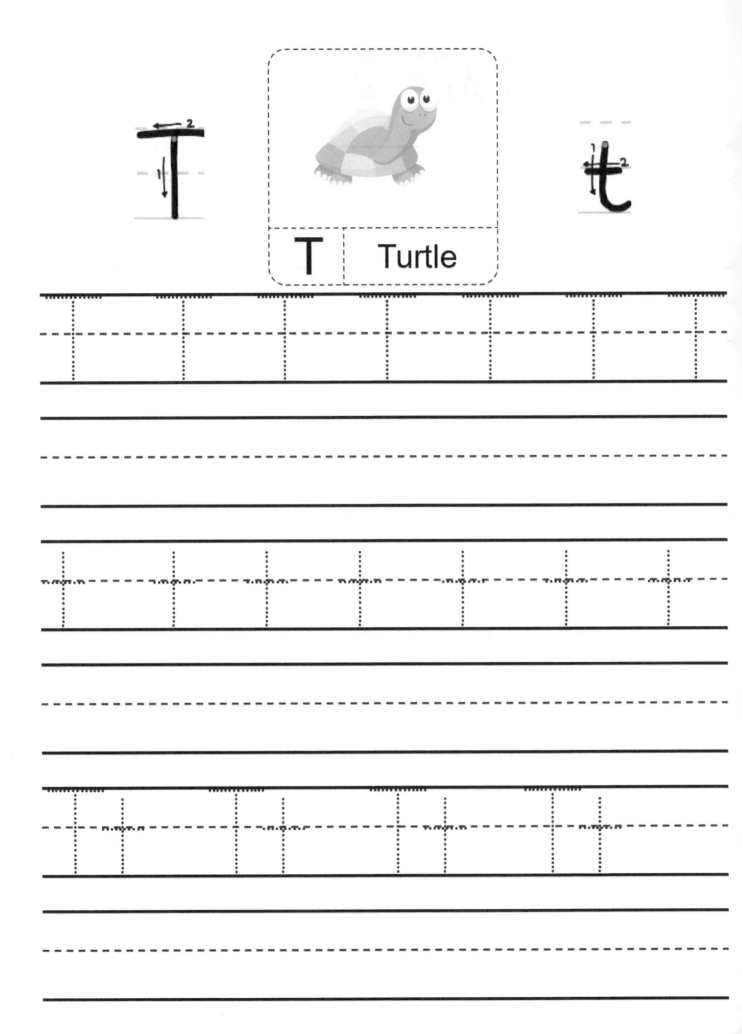

T | Turtle

FREE DRAW

U Unicorn

FREE DRAW

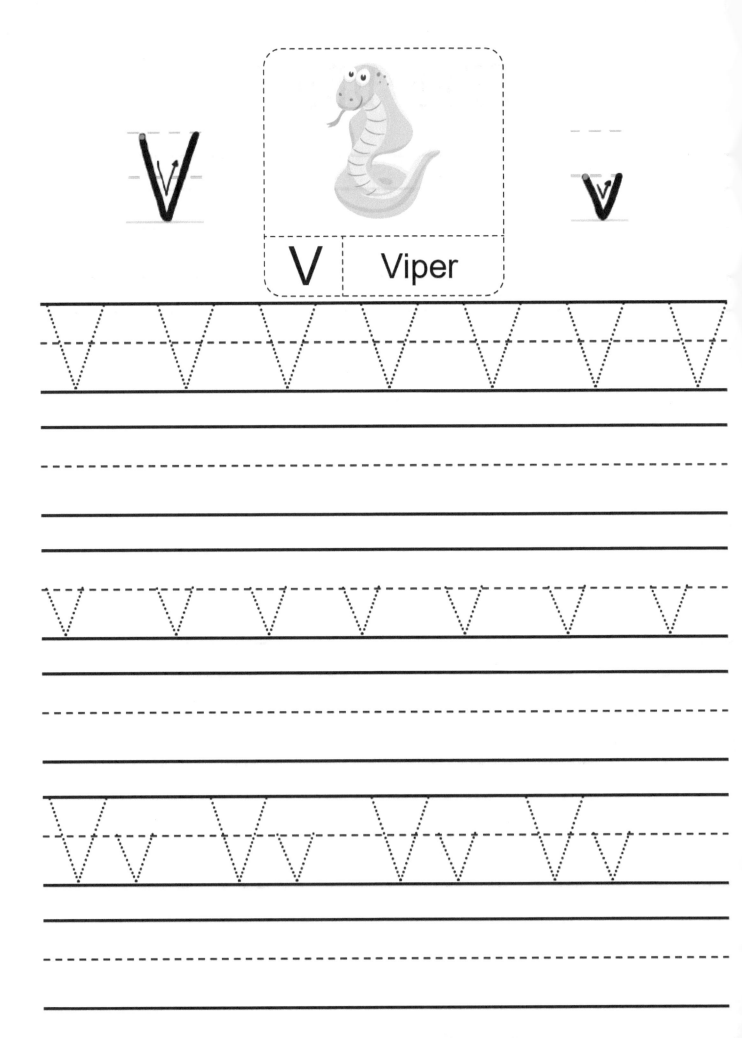

V Viper

FREE DRAW

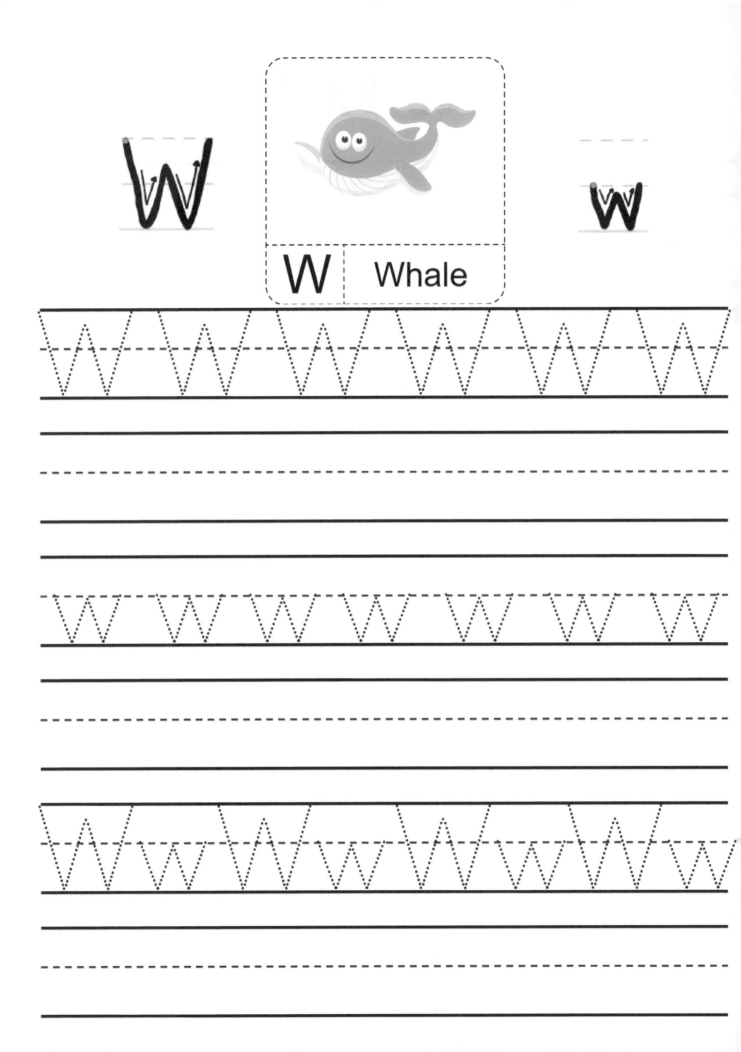

W Whale

FREE DRAW

X | X-ray fish

FREE DRAW

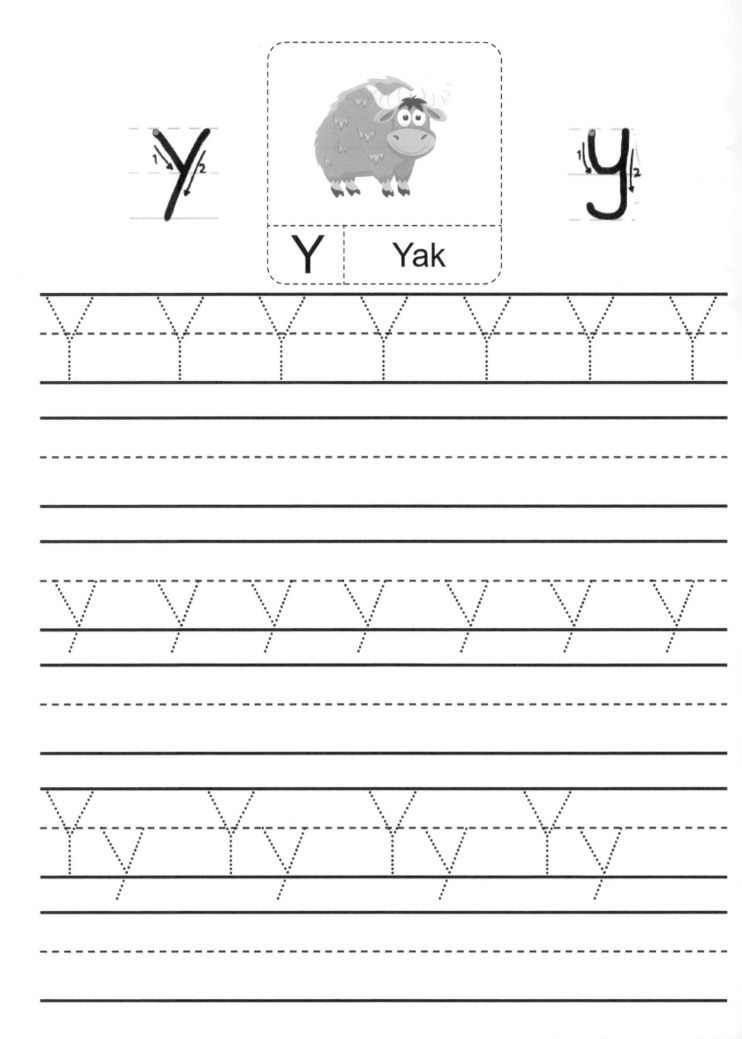

Y   Yak

FREE DRAW

Z

Z | Zebra

z

FREE DRAW

Made in United States
Troutdale, OR
01/25/2024